Lyrical Foreplay

Lyrical Foreplay

Lawrence Anthony

Outskirts Press, Inc.
Denver, Colorado

Lyrical Foreplay

V1.0 R1.0

Outskirts Press, Inc.
http://www.outskirtspress.com

ISBN: 978-1-4327-5814-1

PRINTED IN THE UNITED STATES OF AMERICA

Table of Contents

Lyrical Foreplay

Amour

I love you so much
That my whole existence is you
Depends on you
Evolves around you
I can't live without you
Breathe without you
Until you came into my life
I knew no love had no purpose
Had no meaning
No hope
No idea that your love
Could mean so much to me

About Love

Love is a powerful four letter word.
A verb.
It does not confound or dumbfound.
It is understanding, discreet, and does not cheat.
It is unmitigated and unadulterated.
Love never doubts, fears, nor dies
It is clear as the blue sky.
It does not lie, mystify, nor belie
Love overcomes foolish pride.
It is contagious and patient and gracious.
It is what it is and does what it does.

Beautiful Soul

Sometimes in life we experience the impossible
Sometimes we do the unthinkable
But when a beautiful soul comes into our lives
We're never the same
We're forever changed
Sometimes who we think is Ms. Right or Mr. Right
Is the wrong person
And sometimes a person can be God sent
And make the right imprint
But we overlook them
For some minor flaw
She too dark
She's trailer park
He's lame
She's plain
His nose is too wide
She has a huge back side

Vintage

Baby I'm just thinking of you
And all the things you do
To get me in the mood
With just one look
Into your eyes and at your hip and thighs
Makes me salute and rise
In my mind
I've undressed you
A thousand times
Gently I kissed you
Aiming not to neglect or
Miss any part of you
Truly you are a work of art
A Picasso.
And as our bodies mesh
In an explosion of heat
And sheer ecstasy
I stroke you rhythmically
While you caress me
Baby you feel
So soft and wet
And as I ride
Your sea of love so skillfully
You fulfill me and thrill me
And when darkness turns into light
I rise to see your delight
For I am more into you
Than you are into your self

Paradise

I met this beautiful Caribbean girl
On the white sands of the Malabar Beach
On the island of Saint Lucia
She was my dream come true
She had long locks
That came midway down her curvaceous back
Her eyes were the color of honey
She had on a red and white bathing suit
With a sarong wrapped around her waist
I smiled at her and she smiled back
Her smile was radiant and warm like the sun
She danced with me
So effortlessly so free
Her hips swayed back and forth
Like a palm tree in a breeze
We danced all night long
To love songs
Then she took me to this beautiful place
A quiet place
A place where lovers go
Where waterfalls gush
From the mouth of a volcano
And where lovers take long baths
In hot spring mineral waters

Lyrical Foreplay

Baby I must confess
You're the best
You're the teacher
You make the test
You give the grade
How do you rate my lyrical foreplay

Since I'm a loyal student
Do I get the home schooling
The one on one special treatment

You've heard how I rave about you
How I care about you
How I can't live without you

Is it a sin
To have you again and again
Melt in my mouth like a piece of chocolate

You are the beauty
And I am the beast
Can I feast on your rich cultivated land
You say that's nasty
But I say that's ecstasy
This is only for the grown and sexy
So let's not pretend
You don't want me
As much as I want you

So baby come closer
So I can get another dose of you
You taste so good
You should be a spice on the shelf
But I'm selfish
That's why I can't share you
With anybody else

One Issue

There's just one issue
I'm missing you
You say I was tryin to control you
I say no
I was just tryin to get to know the real you
We got just one issue
I'm missing you
I want you to come home
Where you belong
I know I messed up
I accept responsibility for my indiscretions
Let's forget about the past
And putting me on blast
Don't hate me
Cause you help to make me
So don't try to recreate me
And if you can't take me back
I'll understand
I realize now
I must let you go
To find me

I Adore You

You've touched my heart
And felt my pain
You stood by me quietly
In the midst of my rain
That's why I adore you
And want to explore u
You are the epitome of beauty
So pretty and poised and personable
So magnificent and magnetic
So tempting and titillating and tantalizing
So sultry and sweet and succulent
So -so edible and incredible
Is what you are

Woman

A woman is a gift and a blessin.
A prized possession.
She relishes trinkets
And to hear your innermost secrets.
Giving , loving, kind and divine.
Gentle, loyal, respectful and sweet.
Vivacious, honest, trustworthy and meek.
Woman a gem to find
More precious than lost treasure.

Mister Good Bar

Hello this is Mr. Good Bar
And I have a message for Reese Cup
Now that mars is behind bars
And he played you for a dummy
Don't be Bitter Honey
Cause I'll be your new Nutty Buddy
As long as you break me off a piece of that Kit Kat
We can cuddle and gaze at the stars in the sky
And explore the Milky Way
If you let me put my Butter Fingers
Into your Chunky monkey

Infinite Love

Today we celebrate the undeniable
And pliable love of two becoming one
A love that is real as the firmament of Heaven
A love fresh as the air we breathe
Deep as the blue sea
A love that is not comparable to any

Wife honor your king more than things
Husband love and nurture your beautiful flower

Be mindful to pray
And acknowledge the Lord in all you do
So that His light will continue to shine bright in your lives
Here and thereafter
Shower each other with infinite love
And watch love bloom and grow

Beautiful Flower

Who can resist the beauty of her
So pure so clean
The aesthetics of her beauty
I cannot compare to a person, place, or thing
The smell of her natural herbs
So pleases my sense of being
My face is like a child deceitfully spry
As she walks by
I weaken like a steam engine losing power
As I beheld my beautiful flower

Love

Love walked out on me so abruptly
I never thought it would corrupt me
Like the sun it faded on me
Loneliness became me
So sadly
Now my heart aches so badly
I can't sleep at night
Missing our pillow fights

How could you pray with me
Break bread with me
Then betray me
How could you profess your love for me
Come up with me
Then degrade me
I ponder these questions
While I'm sitting here sex texting you

I miss the scent of you
The touch of you
The sex of you
I miss your smile
Your impeccable style
The laughter with you
The witty words of you

That's why I keep texting you
And singing your praise
Wanting to run my fingers
Through your braids

Vicissitudes of Life

Rainwater purifies earth's flower bed
Lillie's die young in arid, desert like place
The roar of an angry sea lion
Sends billowing waves crashing ashore
A cool autumn zephyr sweeps across torrid plains
Tepid waters flow ever so endlessly down stream
Each day steep hills appear harder to climb
Darkness comes an obscures one's mind
Yet high above the crescent moon
Everlasting hope looms

The Morning After

The morning after day breaks
I put on my new face as I awake
I stretch forth my arms like branches
I'm erect like a tree
I wax bold
Got no time for wavering
I'm active not reactive
Can you see the newness of my eyes
How they radiate
Can you feel the rhythm of my heart
How it palpitates
What I believe
I can achieve
What I set my sights on
Is within my grasp
What I do will be magnified
Baring much fruit

Oak Tree

Oh how it would be
To have roots like a big Oak tree
Then no one could easily move me
Steadfast is what I would be
And when others look at this face of mine
Beauty is the epitome of me
With arms stretched forth so high to the sky
No one could tell me
I couldn't achieve nor succeed

Still Standing

My mind has encountered endless wars and battles
Of enemy attacks in hostile lands
And I conquered them all

My reputation has traveled life's rugged road
Wearily and fadelessly
Into the abyss of
Degradation and humiliation
Not knowing if I was going to make it through
The slanderous attacks
But God navigated my way back

My body has withstood
The constant battering and badgering
Of turbulent winds
And tumultuous rains
And still I stand like a rock

Wake Up

Hey I'm talking to you!
Rebel without a cause.
Did I stutter, stop or pause?
How are you going to be militant
Staggering red eyes bent ?
Negro please!
My children don't eat no government cheese.

Brotha you need a reality check.
Cause your life is shipwrecked.
To sell crack is whack.
Smack!

If we want to bring forth real change
And stop the flow of drugs
And curtail the cycle of violence.
Then we have got to reeducate
And rededicate our selves to the cause
Of uplifting our race.

Let's stop hating and glamorizing thuggism
And use our creatism
To promote capitalism.

Sisters stop selling your bodies
For a blow.
Don't you know you're a African queen
Living a nightmare
Not thee American dream?

The Laments of Rose

Ssh! Listen to the laments of a rose.
When it's surrounded by dandelions and rogues
And involuntarily exposed to the wrong elements.
Picture biceps the size of a python
Wrapped around it's neck.
See how it withers away if left unchecked.
A beautiful red rose
In the middle of an unkempt garden.

Moon Struck

The moon pierces through my blinds.
I ponder if it's a sign.
With moon struck eyes, I'm hypnotized.
So mysteriously, so eerie, so benign!
The moon's light shines bright on me.
Have you ever wondered in amazement
The many moon faces
Or how they alternate places
Or how night yields to day
Or how the moon just scurries away?

I Can

I believe I can achieve
My goals and dreams
Because confidence and faith in GOD
And my talents and abilities
We're instilled in me at an early age
Greatness is destined for me
Because GOD is the architect
He designed and planned it
My mother prayed it
And my father stated it
I can be all that I can be
In spite of my enemies
If I work hard and focus
And follow my dreams

A Brighter Tomorrow

Vagabonds wander aimlessly through the streets
In stench and soiled and tattered clothing
Seeking to satisfy their restless souls
Hoping for a brighter tomorrow.
Criminals wax increasingly bolder.
Winters in Chicago get colder.
People seek solace from the scorching summer heat
But find little or no relief.
Opportunistic robbers and thieves!
Winos congregate on street corners drinking cheap wine
And reminisce about the good times.
Urine reeks in lobbies of project high rises.
Cops pose as criminals in disguises.
Inflation is sky high!
Crabby old ladies grip their purses ever so tightly
As I walk by.
Project elevators are always broke.
Hypes in hallways getting high off coke.
America's solution to the drug epidemic
Is to just say o to dope.
Children living in squalor.
The decline of the mighty dollar.
The millennium nears.
Rumors fall on deaf ears.

The New World Order
Nuclear arms hoarder.
Rival gangs toss up signs.
It's summertime.
Urban blight!
White flight!
Children out all night!
Sirens and lights flashing!
Residents and police clashing!
Self hate and date rape.
Genocide and gay pride.
Racism, discrimination and mis-education.
Economic, social and political injustice.
Dirty politicians.
Adverse conditions .
Black on black crime.
It's all a conspiracy by design.
Infrastructure crumbling.
Children on dirty mattresses tumbling.
Public housing residents living on top of toxic waste.
Public school students being taught
At a buggy and carriage pace.
Steep hills.
Hmm! A golf course on land fills.
I ponder what these environmentalist are thinking.

Budget deficit increasing.
Welfare and aid reform.
In the black community one parent households are the norm.
The O.J. civil trial.
Conservative and alternative lifestyles.
Thousands of apathetic voters.
Drug dealers becoming rap promoters.
Land grabbing.
Back stabbing.
Gang bangers fighting over land
They could never own
Just claim and control.
Undermanned border patrols.
Immigration issues.
Government misuse.
Obama mania.
Human bombing insania
The Bulls held onto their sixth prize.
While projects are being razed.
Tiger woods wins the Masters.
The Katrina and Haiti disasters.
Princess Diana and Dodi Fayed express terms of endearment.
But to their own detriment.

Heaven Bound

I quest for a better place
High above the earth's cavities
Above the indigo sky
Beyond distant galaxies
Far away from petty thieves
A place intricate like the universe
Bountiful and peaceful and diverse
A beautiful paradise is what I envision
Someplace where celestial beings sheen
And phantom like spirits sheen
Patiently I await my wings
For I am God's offspring
Heaven so close to my heart
Yet ever so far

One with the Son

When I am transformed
From this magnificent and majestic earthly vessel
And my jovial spirit is set free
Look to the eastern star that shines so bright
In the night afar
Nether be sad nor glum
For I am one with the Son
I fought a good fight
Against a formidable foe
One in which I could
Neither defend against nor control
Everyday I struggled for
The liberation of my soul
I endured life's endless perils
And when you see me soaring
Like an eagle towards the Son
I'm going home...

Haters

Examine cats how they move so sleek
Unfazed by life's valley's or peaks
Listen to the cries of the black cat
How it is hated on by racist
And power hungry cats
Check out how brown cats
Are not considered as repulsive
As black cats
So they are eased into the mainstream of society
By so called liberal cats
There are mellow yellow cats
Some cool white cats
Some good cats
Some bad ones too
Some are unattached
While some cling
Then there are some hater cats
Which are the worst kind of cats
Even worst than rats
And you know how everyone hates rats

Weary Feet

Mister I'se tired!
I've been standing on my feet for an hour
Waiting for you to take me home.
The sun's a glarin.
White folk are starin.
And making threatening racial epithets.
But I'm not afraid.
I made my peace with God.
Let em talk boisterously.
Let em act foolishly and belligerently.
But I shall not be moved from this seat.
I'se tired and I paid my just dues.
Now they can call me a defiant old negro
Or a stubborn old fool.
They can even jail or beat me for breaking the rules.
But I shall not be moved from this bus seat by choice,
Except by force.

Just Cause

When you fight
Let it be for a just and worthy cause
For a cause that does not elicit shame
Nor seeks fame
A cause that may require martyrdom
To right a wrong
Not a cause to belong
Fight and fight
With all of your might
Kill or be killed
But let it be for just and worthy cause

Misdeeds of the Past

How can I forget
That my ancestors came over
On slave ships not yachts
They were kidnapped including small tots.
And shackled together hand and feet.
And herded like cattle through the street.
An African Kingdom under siege
By pillagers and thieves.
Families were torn apart
And scattered like dust in a breeze.
Sold in the open markets.
Forced to pick cotton.
Born to be free.
But forcibly led into captivity.
Economically exploited and physically owned
Easily distinguished because of their skin tone.
They sung and danced to a rhythmic African beat
Seven days a week in fierce summer heat.
Victimized, brutalized and viciously whipped and beaten
Raped, lynched and inhumanely treated!

Dirty Faces

I've seen men and women in high places
With dirty stoned faces
Fall like disgraced angels from Heaven
Get caught in the webs of deceit
Then get bound by their feet

Be Mindful

I relish the eloquence of speech
And the fanciful ways in which sermons are preached
And how words just roll off the tongue so effortlessly.
Preachers be mindful not to breach the word you teach!

I have a great zeal for poetry and knowledge
And I emphasize to others
The importance of paying God homage.
Politicians be mindful to support the education
Of minds rather than build more prisons to confine!

I marvel at science and technological inventions
And all the hoopla surrounding presidential conventions.
Scientist be mindful that if you err in your thinking
Not to put a veil over the truth your seeking!

I envision a world free of bigoted phobias,
A place so beautiful, so bountiful, so brotherly...a utopia.
Dreamers be mindful to cherish your dreams,
For dreams get blown away like dust in a breeze.

Drunk with Power

Drunk with power
Like the Eiffel tower
Constantly watching over shoulders
With disdainful eyes and pride
Virtually unbearable
Boisterous in talk
Swaggering in walk
Fanatical and ever so melodramatical
An undaunted cynic an tireless critic
Given a title instead of a horses bridle

Ghetto

In everyday life
Sharks devour small defenseless fishes
Dogs chase tail all day while puppies wail
Leeches cling
Nightingales sing their lungs out
Hoping to become the next American Idol
Young jack rabbits are always in a hurry
Scurrying about town with their hand held's
Trying to get into
God knows what
Turtles move at a slow pace
Lepers are becoming an extinct race
Ants plan
Vouchers land
Pigs wallow
Pythons swallow
Herds scatter
Lions capture and batter

Eagles fly instinctively
While zebras have constant conflicts with their identity
Groggy bears hibernate from the coldest winter
Skunks offend
Hyenas grin
Snakes meander in a tornado like pattern
Leaving a path of shattered dreams
Golden retrievers
Eager little beavers
Beautiful swans
Sly foxes
Young wild horses run amok from dusk to dawn
In urban cities all across America
Causing death and destruction
While boisterous roosters awake dreamy eyes
To the morning sunrise

21 Questions

1. Why are we still in bondage when our ancestors were set free?
2. Why do men love their rides?
3. Why do gays and lesbians have more pride?
4. Why is black love being eroded?
5. Why is gangster rap being promoted?
6. Why can't we the people get a bailout in this recession?
7. Why are shoes an obsession for women?
8. Why did MJ's doctor give him all those pills?
9. Why can't doctors cure our ills?
10. Why do so many marriages fail?
11. Why are jails filled with black females and males?
12. Why is racism and sexism systemic?
13. Why is AIDS a black epidemic?
14. Why do people gossip on bossip?
15. Why are some people so damn ignorant and races?
16. Why are public defenders boggled down with so many criminal cases?
17. Why do some people put their personal business on face book?
18. Why are some politicians crooks?
19. Why can't Americans find work?
20. Why are corporate executives given so many perks?
21. Why won't the U.S. do something about the atrocities and poverty occurring in Africa?

Consequences

What do you say to nappy heads in do rags
Who wear saggy pants
And who don't care about their hygiene and appearance
Because there's no parental guidance and interference?

How do you appeal to a thugs intellect when you can't relate with them
And you don't speak their dialect?

What do you say to an unruly and unmotivated teen
In Rocawear jeans
Who only cares about hustling and green
And won't go to school or pick up a book?

What do you say to hard heads
With smart mouths who have low self esteem
Who are promiscuous, smoke weed,
And have unprotected sex?

LaVergne, TN USA
05 August 2010
192272LV00001B/5/P

9 781432 758141